D1764828

congrats, MOMMA ON YOUR *exciting* NEW JOURNEY!

We love and serve a God who desires to talk to us daily. The gift of prayer allows us direct access to the creator of life, which is amazing in and of itself. But not only that, He listens to us when we cry out to him; in joy or sadness, fear or peace, desperation or praise. No prayer is too small and God will never turn his ear away from you. As you begin this new season of parenthood, remember that God wants to be a present and loving companion to you. Lift up your voice to him.

weeks 1-4

Whether you have been trying to get pregnant or it took you by surprise, God was already hard at work knitting together your baby from day one. The tiny embryo growing inside you has an entire outline for everything about them, from their hair color to eye color and even parts of their personality! All of which will be completely unique to them. This week give glory to our God who truly is the great artist! Praise God from whom ALL blessings flow.

Jeremiah 1:5 - Before I formed you in the womb I knew you, before you were born I set you apart.

James 1:17 - Every good and perfect gift is from above, coming down from the Father of the heavenly lights, who does not change like shifting shadows.

week 5

Even though your baby is only the size of an apple seed, their carefully designed heart has already started beating. God created us with a yearning for Him within our hearts, and because of that, we will always feel like there is something missing if we are living life apart from Christ. As your child gets older, plenty of people will try and convince them that the things of this world can take the place of Jesus. Pray that your little one will fill the "Jesus-shaped hole" in their heart with things of the Lord instead of temptations here on earth.

Ephesians 2:8 - For it is by grace you have been saved, through faith—and this is not from yourselves, it is the gift of God.

Romans 3:23 - For all have sinned and fall short of the glory of God.

week 6

The eyes, nose, and ears that you will spend so much time kissing are all beginning to take form. While your child will most likely look like one of their parents, remember that they were FIRST made in the likeness of Christ. Everything about us was created to reflect and give glory back to God. While we will never be perfect or sinless here on earth, we continually strive to be more like Jesus so that those around us would be drawn to His life changing love, too. Pray that what stands out most when people see your child is not their physical looks, but the Spirit of the Lord that shines through them.

Ephesians 5:1-2 - Follow God's example, therefore, as dearly loved children and walk in the way of love, just as Christ loved us and gave himself up for us as a fragrant offering and sacrifice to God.

week 7

This week you may begin to feel nauseous or dizzy depending on your pregnancy. Even though it can be difficult, know that this is a sign of health and growth in your child! Your baby's brain is forming this week and their brain waves can be recorded. Pray that the Lord would instill a passion for learning the Word of God in your child and that they would use their intelligence to serve the Kingdom by teaching others about Jesus.

Psalm 119:11 - I have hidden your word in my heart that I might not sin against you.

Proverbs 2:1-5 - My son, if you accept my words and store up my commands within you, turning your ear to wisdom and applying your heart to understanding—indeed, if you call out for insight and cry aloud for understanding, and if you look for it as for silver and search for it as for hidden treasure, then you will understand the fear of the Lord and find the knowledge of God.

week 8

This week your baby's hands and feet are growing and forming from their budding arms and legs. Even though you can't feel it yet, your baby (which is the size of a kidney bean) is jumping and moving inside of you. Pray that your baby will be the hands and feet of Jesus and serve those in need around them. Pray that they will be so filled with the joy of the Holy Spirit that they cannot help but dance!

Ephesians 6:7 - Serve wholeheartedly, as if you were serving the Lord, not people.

Philippians 4:4 - Rejoice in the Lord always. I will say it again: Rejoice!

week 9

This week your baby's eyes are fully formed. Pray that if you have a son, he would be able to turn his eyes from the lust and temptation that the world presents. Pray that if you have a daughter, she would not assess herself based on the world's standard of beauty, but rather what the Lord declares is beautiful.

Matthew 5:28 - But I tell you that anyone who looks at a woman lustfully has already committed adultery with her in his heart.

1 Peter 3:3-4 - Your beauty should not come from outward adornment, such as elaborate hairstyles and the wearing of gold jewelry or fine clothes. Rather, it should be that of your inner self, the unfading beauty of a gentle and quiet spirit, which is of great worth in God's sight.

week 10

This week your baby is swallowing fluid and growing nails. Blood cells are being produced in the kidneys and are flowing through their body. Pray that your child would one day understand the sacrifice of Christ's blood on the cross and that they would accept the gift of salvation. Pray that the Lord would also guide you in the gospel conversations that you will have with them one day.

1 John 1:7-9 - But if we walk in the light, as he is in the light, we have fellowship with one another, and the blood of Jesus, his Son, purifies us from all sin. If we claim to be without sin, we deceive ourselves and the truth is not in us. If we confess our sins, he is faithful and just and will forgive us our sins and purify us from all unrighteousness.

week 11

This week your baby may be having hiccups (which you will feel in the weeks to come) and their tiny tooth buds are forming. In the not-too-distant future your baby will be using their teeth to eat and they might reject some of the healthy foods that you offer. Just like with babies, we don't always crave what is holy, sometimes we get drawn in by what we think will feel best in the moment. Pray that your child will learn to discern between the things that are glorifying to God, and the lies that Satan will try to feed them.

1 Peter 5:8 - Be alert and of sober mind. Your enemy the devil prowls around like a roaring lion looking for someone to devour.

John 10:10 - The thief comes only to steal and kill and destroy; I have come that they may have life, and have it to the full.

week 12

This week your baby's reflexes have developed and they can respond to touch or prodding. This takes the coordination of their brain, nervous system, muscles, tendons, bones, plus tons of other minuscule body functions. The way that God has designed humans to grow is absolutely miraculous, and many women never get to share in this amazing experience. So this week praise God for the blessing He has given you in the form of pregnancy.

Psalm 106:1-2 - Praise the Lord. Give thanks to the Lord, for he is good; his love endures forever. Who can proclaim the mighty acts of the Lord or fully declare his praise?

Psalm 127:3-5 - Children are a heritage from the Lord, offspring are a reward from him. Like arrows in the hands of a warrior are children born in one's youth. Blessed is the man whose quiver is full of them. They will not be put to shame when they contend with their opponents in court.

week 13

This week fingerprints have formed on your baby's fingertips. Your little one's fingerprints are unique to them alone; no one else will have the exact same identity as your precious child! Unfortunately, Satan has a way of trying to convince us that everyone needs to look the same and chase after the things of this world. Pray that your child would not seek to find their identity in worldly success or acceptance, but instead would find their identity in Christ. Pray that they will have confidence to walk into this confusing world with a foundation built firmly on Jesus.

John 15:5 - I am the vine; you are the branches. If you remain in me and I in you, you will bear much fruit; apart from me you can do nothing.

2 Corinthians 5:17 - Therefore, if anyone is in Christ, he is a new creation. The old has passed away; behold, the new has come.

week 14

Your baby is now about the size of a lemon and practicing all kinds of facial expressions. They will be using facial muscles to squint, frown, grimace, and maybe even suck their thumb! As your baby is learning how to control different parts of their body, pray that your little one will also learn self-control over their attitude and behavior, even as other children around them may be disobeying.

Philippians 4:8 - Finally, brothers and sisters, whatever is true, whatever is noble, whatever is right, whatever is pure, whatever is lovely, whatever is admirable—if anything is excellent or praiseworthy—think about such things.

James 4:17 - So whoever knows the right thing to do and fails to do it, for him it is sin.

week 15

This week your baby's eyes become sensitive to light. If you were to shine a flashlight at your belly they would reflexively move away from the brightness to shield their eyes. We see the same response from Moses in Exodus 3 when God appears to him in the fiery bush. And again in Acts 9 when Saul (later renamed Paul) was met on the road near Damascus by a shining light and the voice of the Lord. Pray that your baby would understand the almightly power and glory of God, and that they would reflexively bow in awe at the magnificent splender of our creator God.

Read all of Exodus 3 - There the angel of the Lord appeared to him in flames of fire from within a bush...Take off your sandals, for the place where you are standing is holy ground." Then he said, "I am the God of your father, the God of Abraham, the God of Isaac and the God of Jacob." At this, Moses hid his face.

Read all of Acts 9 -As he journeyed he came near Damascus, and suddenly a light shone around him from heaven. Then he fell to the ground.

week 16

This week your baby is about the size of an avocado, but in the next few weeks they will go through a growth spurt and double in size! This is going to be hard work for your baby, but that is not a bad thing. God wants us to be hard workers, so pray that your child would have a willing attitude to work hard at everything they do in life.

Colossians 3:23 - Whatever you do, work at it with all your heart, as working for the Lord.

Philippians 2:14-16a - Do everything without grumbling or arguing, so that you may become blameless and pure, "children of God without fault in a warped and crooked generation. Then you will shine among them like stars in the sky as you hold firmly to the word of life.

week 17

Today your baby's skeleton is changing from soft cartilage into bone. Not only that, but the umbilical cord, which supplies all the life-giving nutrients to your baby, is growing stronger and thicker. As your child grows stronger physically, pray that they will also understand what it means to be strong spiritually, and to understand what it means to have faith without sight.

Hebrews 11:1 - Now faith is confidence in what we hope for and assurance about what we do not see.

Luke 17:5-6 - The apostles said to the Lord, "Increase our faith!" He replied, "If you have faith as small as a mustard seed, you can say to this mulberry tree, 'Be uprooted and planted in the sea,' and it will obey you.

week 18

This week your baby is flexing their arms and legs all the time and their ears have moved into their final position. Pray that your child would have ears to hear the call of God's irresistible grace. The world will create a lot of noise and distraction around your child that can draw them away from the voice of the Lord. But the beauty of the Holy Spirit is that God is always near! At any moment we can cry out to him and He is with us. Pray that your baby would always carry with them the love and faithfulness of Jesus Christ.

Proverbs 3:3 - Let love and faithfulness never leave you; bind them around your neck, write them on the tablet of your heart.

Ephesians 5:2 -Walk in the way of love, just as Christ loved us and gave himself up for us as a fragrant offering and sacrifice to God.

week 19

This week your baby is growing hair. They are also beginning to have nerve connections to all five of their senses: touch, sight, sound, smell, and taste. As your baby fine-tunes each of these physical senses, pray that they would also one day be strong in the senses of the Spirit: love, joy, peace, patience, kindness, goodness, faithfulness, gentleness and self-control. Take time to pray for EACH of the fruits of the Spirit individually.

Galatians 5:22-23a - But the fruit of the Spirit is love, joy, peace, patience, kindness, goodness, faithfulness, gentleness, and self-control.

Ephesians 5:9 - For the fruit of the light consists in all goodness, righteousness and truth.

week 20

This week your baby is the size of a banana and if you want to, you will be able to tell if it's a boy or girl! It can be easier to pray for your baby once you know the gender, so be extra intentional this week to pray for their specific gender needs. Men and women were both made in God's image and are equally cherished as His children; and yet, he also chose to make us distinct, both in creation and in roles. Pray that your child would know and value God's vision for the uniqueness of both men and women.

Read all of Titus 2:1-8 ...Similarly, encourage the young men to be self-controlled... In your teaching show integrity, seriousness and soundness of speech that cannot be condemned, so that those who oppose you may be ashamed because they have nothing bad to say about us...

Read all of Proverbs 31:10-31 ...A wife of noble character who can find? She is worth far more than rubies. Her husband has full confidence in her and lacks nothing of value. She brings him good, not harm, all the days of her life...

week 21

This week your baby is having more consistent wake and sleep cycles throughout the day. Not only that, but their tongue is now fully formed, so pray that your child would only use their words to build others up and not to tear them down. Pray that your little one would think before speaking, being patient enough to hold their tongue and learn to be a good listener.

1 Thessalonians 5:11 - Therefore encourage one another and build each other up, just as in fact you are doing.

Proverbs 29:20 - Do you see someone who speaks in haste? There is more hope for a fool than for them.

week 22

This week your little one weighs almost a pound! Your baby can also hear you talking, reading, or singing to them. Studies have shown that babies in utero will suck their thumb more vigorously when hearing their mother's voice. As a parent, your voice will have more of an influence over your child than anyone else's. Pray that your child will always listen and respect the decisions and wisdom of their parents or caregivers.

Ephesians 6:1-3 - Children, obey your parents in the Lord, for this is right. "Honor your father and mother"—which is the first commandment with a promise— "so that it may go well with you and that you may enjoy long life on the earth."

Proverbs 20:11 - Even children are known by the way they act, whether their conduct is pure, and whether it is right.

week 23

By this point in your pregnancy you can most likely feel your baby moving around inside of you. God creates this special connection that your baby will share with only you, which is the beginning of a lifetime bond that we often refer to as "a mother's love." Pray this week that you would be able to show your child what unconditional love looks like. Pray that your baby would be able to love others as you (and as Christ) have loved them first.

1 John 4:18 - Such love has no fear, because perfect love expels all fear. If we are afraid, it is for fear of punishment, and this shows that we have not fully experienced his perfect love.

John 15:12–13 - This is my commandment: Love each other in the same way I have loved you. There is no greater love than to lay down one's life for one's friends.

week 24

This week your baby is officially considered viable, meaning that if they were to be born right now it is possible that they could survive outside the womb. Part of this is due to their lung development and being able to pump air in and out easier. As your baby's lungs continue to grow, pray that they would use their voice to stand up for those who can't stand up for themselves. Pray that your little one would have a sense of justice that guides them to boldly speak up when they see someone who needs help, just like our Savior, Jesus Christ.

Psalm 11:7 - For the Lord is righteous, he loves justice; the upright will see his face.

Micah 6:8 - He has shown you, O mortal, what is good. And what does the Lord require of you? To act justly and to love mercy and to walk humbly with your God.

week 25

This week your baby is getting much bigger, weighing 1.5lbs and stretching to 15 inches! Most of this weight comes from organs, muscle, and bone mass. Your baby is also starting to look more like a newborn, even though they are still pretty lean (like an ear of corn). As your baby's body continues to grow every day, pray that they will also grow in a personal relationship with God. Pray that your child will see Him as "daddy" and treasure the special relationship they have together.

Psalm 63:8 - I cling to you; your right hand upholds me.

1 John 3:1 - See what great love the Father has lavished on us, that we should be called children of God! And that is what we are! The reason the world does not know us is that it did not know him.

week 26

This week your baby is practicing breathing motions by inhaling and exhaling amniotic fluid. This is so important because it readies them for the first breath they'll take once they are born. Just as your baby knows they need to breathe in life-giving oxygen without question, they also need to have faith in the life-giving power of the Cross. Because Jesus died on the cross for our sins, nothing can separate us from him; we don't need to fear our circumstances because we know He is always with us. Pray this week that your baby will have a faith that moves mountains, a faith that is unshakeable.

Matthew 17:20 - Truly I tell you, if you have faith as small as a mustard seed, you can say to this mountain, 'Move from here to there,' and it will move. Nothing will be impossible for you."

Romans 8:38–39 - For I am convinced that neither death nor life, neither angels nor demons, neither the present nor the future, nor any powers, neither height nor depth, nor anything else in all creation, will be able to separate us from the love of God that is in Christ Jesus our Lord.

week 27

Your baby's brain continues to grow rapidly and their hearing is becoming even more fine-tuned. Your little one is at the point now where they recognize your voice and possibly your partner's, and may even respond with kicks and wiggles! These little moves are a sign of your child's excitement and contentment to be a part of you, which is a good reminder to pray that as they grow they will live a life of contentment. Pray that no matter the circumstance, your child would have the ability be satisfied in Christ alone.

Philippians 4:11-13 - I am not saying this because I am in need, for I have learned to be content whatever the circumstances. I know what it is to be in need, and I know what it is to have plenty. I have learned the secret of being content in any and every situation, whether well fed or hungry, whether living in plenty or in want. I can do all this through him who gives me strength.

week 28

This week your baby is about 2.5 pounds and has eyelashes and eyebrows! As their muscle tonc improves this week, you may also start to notice your baby giving you many more (and stronger) kicks. Even though this is the only thing your baby can be "generous" with at this point, pray that they would one day be generous to others. Pray that they would have a willingness to share toys and other things, with the knowledge that we can't store up treasures here on earth.

1 Timothy 6:18-19 - Command them to do good, to be rich in good deeds, and to be generous and willing to share. In this way they will lay up treasure for themselves as a firm foundation for the coming age, so that they may take hold of the life that is truly life.

Proverbs 19:17 - Whoever is kind to the poor lends to the Lord, and he will reward them for what they have done.

week 29

This week your baby is about the size of a butternut squash and is growing like crazy! Their muscles, lungs, bones and brain are developing at a rapid pace and you will need to be taking in plenty of milk, protein, vitamin C, and folic acid to keep up with their growing nutritional needs (so take your prenatal vitamin!). As you are helping to meet your baby's physical needs, pray that you will also be able to help your little one understand their spiritual needs. Pray that you and your family could teach them about our need for God and the sweetness of the free gift we have in salvation.

Proverbs 22:6 - Start children off on the way they should go, and even when they are old they will not turn from it.

Deuteronomy 6:6-7 - These commandments that I give you today are to be on your hearts. Impress them on your children. Talk about them when you sit at home and when you walk along the road, when you lie down and when you get up.

week 30

This is a week where many of the Lord's tiny details become visible on your baby's body. Your little one can move their eyes from side-to-side and may even reach toward a light source. Not only that, but your baby can already produce tears inside the womb! God tied together the physiological response of tears to an overflow of emotion, ranging from joy to hurt to anger. Pray this week that your child would be tender and overflowing with compassion and mercy for those around them.

Luke 6:36 - Be merciful, just as your Father is merciful.

Colossians 3:12 - Therefore, as God's chosen people, holy and dearly loved, clothe yourselves with compassion, kindness, humility, gentleness and patience.

week 31

This week your baby has grown to the size of a coconut and has gained major control in moving their arms and legs. At this point in your pregnancy it may be getting hard for you to sleep through some of these movements. As you persevere through this last stretch of pregnancy, take the time to pray for your little one as you wait for them to settle down. Pray that your child would develop perseverance in everything they do and have a sense of commitment to the task at hand, particularly whatever the Lord has planned for them.

Hebrews 12:1 - Therefore, since we are surrounded by such a great cloud of witnesses, let us throw off everything that hinders and the sin that so easily entangles. And let us run with perseverance the race marked out for us.

week 32

From here on out you will probably gain about a pound a week until you deliver, with half of that going straight to your baby. Meanwhile, your little one is practicing using their five senses that are all working by now. Research with heart rates have shown that your baby may even have a preference for one style of music over another, so introduce them to your favorite artists and see if your baby has inherited your musical taste! Pray this week that your child would develop a heart of worship, not only by way of singing, but also through prayer, serving, writing, or whatever way they feel most connected to the Lord.

Psalm 95:6 - Come, let us bow down in worship, let us kneel before the Lord our Maker.

Isaiah 12:5 - Sing to the Lord, for he has done glorious things; let this be known to all the world.

week 33

This week your baby has real hair growing and their skin is becoming soft and smooth as they gain more and more weight. They are also perfecting their sucking and swallowing motions in preparation for delivery and life outside the womb. Isn't it crazy that they are preparing for something they don't even know is coming? But even when we are faced with the unknown, God prepares a way for us; he is always in control. Pray this week that your baby would always trust that God has a plan for them, even when they don't understand it.

Jeremiah 29:11 - For I know the plans I have for you," declares the Lord, "plans to prosper you and not to harm you, plans to give you hope and a future.

John 14:3 - And if I go and prepare a place for you, I will come back and take you to be with me that you also may be where I am.

week 34

Your baby weighs almost five pounds and is about 18 inches long. The bones of the skull are hardening, but they are not fused together (they are slightly overlapping), which will make it easier for the baby to pass through the birth canal. Your little one is also starting to sleep in REM cycles with noticeable wake and sleep periods. Pray this week that your baby would not "fall asleep" to what God may try to tell them later in life. Pray that they would be wakeful and listening for the voice of God, even in their day-to-day activities.

Matthew 24:42 - Therefore keep watch, because you do not know on what day your Lord will come.

1 Corinthians 10:31 - So whether you eat or drink or whatever you do, do it all for the glory of God.

1 Peter 2:9 - But you are a chosen people, a royal priesthood, a holy nation, God's special possession, that you may declare the praises of him who called you out of darkness into his wonderful light.

week 35

Now that your baby is over five pounds they won't be doing much flipping, but their kicking movements should still be frequent. Your little one is putting on enough weight to create those adorable dimples on their knees and elbows and their body is starting to regulate temperature. The kidneys are also fully developed and the liver can process waste products. Pray that as your child grows they would be able to sift through all of the excess distractions of this world and instead set their sights on things eternal.

Proverbs 4:25-27 - Let your eyes look straight ahead; fix your gaze directly before you. Give careful thought to the paths for your feet and be steadfast in all your ways. Do not turn to the right or the left; keep your foot from evil.

Philippians 2:15 - So that you may become blameless and pure, "children of God without fault in a warped and crooked generation." Then you will shine among them like stars in the sky.

week 36

Your baby weighs almost six pounds and is over 18 inches long. Their lungs and nervous system are continuing to mature and if your baby was born now, they would most likely have no major health problems other than staying a couple extra days at the hospital while they finish growing. You may be feeling impatient or worried as you approach your due date, so this week's prayer is for both of you. Pray that the Lord would grant you peace and patience as you wait out these last few weeks of pregnancy. Pray that your child would grow strong in these characteristics of the Lord as they get older as well!

2 Thessalonians 3:16 - Now may the Lord of peace himself give you peace at all times and in every way. The Lord be with all of you.

John 16:33 - "I have told you these things, so that in me you may have peace. In this world you will have trouble. But take heart! I have overcome the world."

week 37

Congratulations! You have made it to full term. If you were to deliver today, your baby's lungs should be mature enough to function outside of the womb without any help. But even though you *could* give birth now, every day inside your tummy is still helpful in your baby's growth process. Your little one now also has a firm grasp and it won't be long before you feel that strong, little squeeze around your finger and probably yanking your hair! This week pray that when your child feels weak or lost that they would cry out to the Lord and ask for strength that only He can supply.

Romans 12:12 - Be joyful in hope, patient in affliction, faithful in prayer.

Psalm 22:19- But you, LORD, do not be far from me. You are my strength; come quickly to help me.

week 38

This week your baby weighs almost seven pounds and is 19.5 inches long. You have probably been making guesses about what your baby will look like- what color of hair they will be born with, whose eyes they will have. Keep in mind that it is normal for a baby's hair or eye color to change over the first couple of months; this is all a part of God's creativity! He has made your sweet little one so unique. Pray that your child would be able to embrace all the things that make them special and realize that God has created them perfectly, because our Father makes no mistakes.

Psalm 139:13-16 - For you created my inmost being; you knit me together in my mother's womb. I praise you because I am fearfully and wonderfully made; your works are wonderful, I know that full well. My frame was not hidden from you when I was made in the secret place, when I was woven together in the depths of the earth. Your eyes saw my unformed body; all the days ordained for me were written in your book before one of them came to be.

week 39

Your baby continues to build layers of fat to control body temperature after birth, and because they are about the size of a small watermelon, they have very little room to move. You have probably been receiving weekly checks from your doctor or midwife to see if you are making progress toward going into labor. As you are making preparations to be ready to deliver any day now, pray that your child would also be prepared to represent Christ at any given moment. Pray that they would not waver, but would stand firm in the truth of Christ.

1 Peter 3:15 - But in your hearts revere Christ as Lord. Always be prepared to give an answer to everyone who asks you to give the reason for the hope that you have. But do this with gentleness and respect.

Ephesians 6:19 - Pray also for me, that whenever I speak, words may be given me so that I will fearlessly make known the mystery of the gospel.

week 40

You have officially reached your due date! While you are probably experiencing a mixture of excitement, exhaustion, and frustration, remember that this day is just an estimate and only 5% of babies are actually born on their due date. So take heart! You are not alone in still being pregnant (even though it may feel like it). Use these last few days to finish any cleaning or organizing you want done, and remember that God holds all things in His hands, including the timing of your little one's arrival. Praise Him this week for allowing your baby to reach full-term and relish the last of the kicks you feel from the inside, believe it or not you will miss them!

Isaiah 40:31 - But those who hope in the Lord will renew their strength. They will soar on wings like eagles; they will run and not grow weary, they will walk and not be faint.

Ecclesiastes 8:6 - For there is a proper time and procedure for every matter, though a person may be weighed down by misery.

weeks 41-42

You are probably talking to your care provider about a possible induction or C-section if you don't deliver in the next few days. While your baby is cozy and comfy inside of you, it's important that you are planning and praying about the safest possible delivery. As you await the arrival of your sweet baby, pray that they will learn to go to God in prayer for every situation. Pray that your little one would converse with the Lord throughout the day for little decisions (like their going home outfit) and big decisions (like how and when they will enter the world). Proud of you for making it this far, mamma! Your bundle of joy will be here any day now.

1 Thessalonians 5:16-18 - Rejoice always, pray continually, give thanks in all circumstances; for this is God's will for you in Christ Jesus.

Philippians 4:6 - Do not be anxious about anything, but in every situation, by prayer and petition, with thanksgiving, present your requests to God.

Copyright © 2019 Duncan & Stone Paper Co.
www.duncanandstone.com

All rights reserved. No part of this publication may be
reproduced or transmitted in any from or by any means,
electronic or mechanical, including photocopying and
recording, or by any information storage and retrieval
system, without permission in writing from the author.

Scriptures taken from The Holy Bible,
New International Version®, NIV®, Copyright 1973,
1978, 1984, 2011 by Biblica Inc.® Used by permission.
All rights reserved worldwide.
Printed in China